The
SHERLOCK HOLMES
school of
SELF-DEFENCE

The
SHERLOCK HOLMES
school of
SELF-DEFENCE

The Manly Art of Bartitsu

as used against PROFESSOR MORIARTY

E. W. BARTON-WRIGHT

Ivy Press

First published in the UK in 2011

Ivy Press

210 High Street

Lewes

East Sussex BN7 2NS

United Kingdom

www.ivypress.co.uk

Copyright © Ivy Press Limited 2011

British Library Cataloguing-in-Publication Data

A catalogue record for this book is available from the British Library

ISBN: 978-1-907332-73-9

Ivy Press

This book was conceived, designed, and produced by Ivy Press

Creative Director Peter Bridgewater

Publisher Jason Hook

Art Director Wayne Blades

Senior Editor Jayne Ansell

Text Andrew Kirk

Designer Joanna Clinch

Printed in China

Colour Origination by Ivy Press Reprographics

10 9 8 7 6 5 4 3 2 1

Contents

"We tottered together upon the brink of the fall.
I have some knowledge, however, of baritsu,
or the Japanese system of wrestling, which has
more than once been very useful to me. I slipped
through his grip, and he with a horrible scream
kicked madly for a few seconds and clawed the
air with both his hands. But for all his efforts he
could not get his balance, and over he went.
With my face over the brink I saw him fall for
a long way. Then he struck a rock, bounced off,
and splashed into the water."

Sir Arthur Conan Doyle, *The Empty House* (1903)

Introduction

*When Sir Arthur Conan Doyle was obliged by popular
demand to resurrect his famous detective, Sherlock Holmes,
whom he had consigned to the abyss of the Reichenbach
Falls at the end of THE FINAL PROBLEM in 1894, it was perhaps
not surprising that he turned to the contemporary craze for
martial arts to account for his hero's remarkable escape.
We know from Dr Watson that Holmes was an expert
singlestick player, boxer and swordsman. Nothing then could be
more natural than that he should also turn out to be proficient
in BARITSU, the Japanese system of wrestling, by which means
he was able to prevail over his nemesis, Professor Moriarty, and
reappear miraculously in THE EMPTY HOUSE in 1903.*

Conan Doyle's account is, however, inaccurate
in two respects. In the first place, the name
of the martial art that saves Holmes was not
BARITSU but BARTITSU; and in the second place, though
it was derived from Japanese methods, it was the
invention of an Englishman, who gave the system his
own name – Edward William Barton-Wright. Barton-
Wright was born in India in 1860 to a Scottish mother
and a Northumbrian father, and he was by profession a
consulting engineer. His work took him all around the
world, and it was during an extended period living in

Japan that he became fascinated by jiu-jitsu, and took lessons in the art himself. On his return to London in 1898, Barton-Wright began to develop his new system of self-defence, publishing two articles in PEARSON'S MAGAZINE and opening his Bartitsu Club in Shaftesbury Avenue in 1900. He brought two Japanese experts in jiu-jitsu over to England to teach in the school. Bartitsu was closely based on jiu-jitsu, but combined with it elements of boxing, wrestling, savate (French kick-boxing) and stick-fighting. Barton-Wright claimed that his system was proof against attacks of every kind.

Defence for the gentleman

arton-Wright's system of self-defence met a number of concerns that were dear to the heart of the late Victorian and Edwardian gentleman. Notions of physical culture and muscular Christianity had been current since the mid-nineteenth century, and implied that it was a moral duty for the English gentleman to be a physically robust specimen. The dismay that many commentators expressed in the late 1880s about the increasing physical degeneracy of Englishmen as machines and mechanised transport took the place of manual effort derived in part from this devotion to the idea of MENS SANA IN CORPORE SANO (a healthy mind in a healthy body). Alongside this there was widespread alarm at lurid newspaper accounts of the depredations of violent street gangs – Hooligans in London, Scuttlers in Manchester, Cornermen in Liverpool – whose methods did not answer to English ideas of fair play. In the face of this unmanly onslaught, the gentleman who did not wish to rely on the protection of a revolver (an option which many, in fact, chose during the period around the turn of the century) would be ready to look overseas for methods of self-defence that had a similar disregard for fair play. The Bartitsu Club, however, was by no means the only school of self-defence available. Numerous jiu-jitsu clubs were established, as well as schools that taught the art of stick-fighting, and these were frequented by both men and women. Mrs Edith Garrud famously opened a school of jiu-jitsu and trained 'The Bodyguard', a group of suffragette sympathisers who protected the leaders of the Suffragette Movement from attack during their public appearances. Sadly, this jiu-jitsu boom left Barton-Wright behind. The Bartitsu Club closed in 1902, apparently because of financial difficulties. He fell out with his chief jiu-jitsuka, Yukio Tani, who went to work in the music halls with the strongman William Bankier, and Barton-Wright's system sadly faded into obscurity, its inventor himself dying a pauper in 1951. Nonetheless, thanks to Sherlock Holmes, he has not been entirely lost to posterity, AND HIS SYSTEM IS HERE PRESENTED AS ORIGINALLY EXPOUNDED.

"In this country we are brought up with the idea that there is no more honourable way of settling a dispute than resorting to Nature's weapons, the fists, and to scorn taking advantage of another man when he is down. A foreigner, however, will not hesitate to use a chair, or a beer bottle, or a knife, or anything that comes handy, and if no weapon is available the chances are he would employ what we should consider are underhanded means. It is to meet eventualities of this kind, where a person is confronted suddenly in an unexpected way, that I have introduced a new style of self-defence, which can be very terrible in the hands of a quick and confident exponent."

E. W. Barton-Wright, "The New Art of Self-defence",
Pearson's Magazine (March 1899)

☞ THERE IS NO SOCIAL *occurrence more distasteful than* when a person, either by reason of inebriation or gracelessness, *makes himself unpleasant at a* gathering, particularly when there **ARE LADIES PRESENT.** Where chilly disdain or verbal admonishments are unequal to resolving the situation, *force is* *the only alternative, and it is* desirable to be able to perform **THE NECESSARY OPERATION** with the minimum of fuss and the greatest DEGREE OF EXPEDITION.

CHAPTER 1

How to deal WITH undesirables

Putting a *troublesome man* out of the room: method 1

It will not be necessary to impress upon the reader the importance of knowing how any undesirable visitor may be promptly ejected from a room. Such knowledge is of inestimable service. Two methods may be conveniently described, the first being suited to a person who might be about to strike you.

(Fig. 1) Seize your opponent by the left wrist with your left hand, while raising your right hand to guard your face from a blow. Pull him towards you with your left arm, without altering the position of your legs. Then turn upon your heel and pass your right arm over his upper left arm.

(Fig. 2) You then pass your right hand under his left arm and lock his arm by seizing your own left wrist. By straightening both your arms you will be able to exert such leverage, and to throw such a strain upon his elbow, that you could break it should he attempt to resist. If the leverage be exerted in the proper way, it will also be found that it is quite impossible for your opponent to hit you or to retaliate in any way.

Fig. 1

Fig. 2

Fig. 1

Fig. 2

Putting a *troublesome man* out of the room: method 2

Suppose that an undesirable person should enter your rooms, and that you are anxious to remove him without delay. You find that persuasion and commands alike fail. It may be that he is a bigger man than yourself, and you may hesitate to propel him out of your door by the common method. Should you adopt the following plan your visitor will give you no further trouble.

(Fig. 1) Seize his right wrist with your right hand, turning the inside of his arm upwards. Then step towards him with your left foot, pass your left arm underneath his right upper arm, and seize hold of the lappet of his coat, so as to support your left arm and prevent it from sliding downwards.

(Fig. 2) Now exert downward pressure upon your victim's arm, and with the leverage so obtained you could, if he attempted to resist you, break his arm at the elbow. From this position you will not have the smallest difficulty in ejecting him from the room.

Of course, there are occasions when a blustering and intrusive visitor, even one armed with a hunting-crop, may be dispatched without the use of force, but simply through the deployment of non-sequiturs and unruffled good humour:

"Our door had been suddenly dashed open, and a huge man framed himself in the aperture.

'I am Dr Grimesby Roylott, of Stoke Moran.'

'Indeed, Doctor,' said Holmes blandly.
'Pray take a seat.'

'I will do nothing of the kind.
My stepdaughter has been here. I have traced her.
What has she been saying to you?'

'It is a little cold for the time of year,' said Holmes.

'What has she been saying to you?'
screamed the old man furiously.
'But I have heard that the crocuses promise well,'
continued my companion, imperturbably …
'Your conversation is most entertaining.
When you go out, close the door,
for there is a decided draught.'"

Sir Arthur Conan Doyle, *The Speckled Band* (1892)

☞ AN ATTACK FROM THE REAR

MAY BE CONSIDERED

the most unnerving, and for that

reason the most common, of the

assaults that may be suffered by a

GENTLEMAN

IN THE MORE INSALUBRIOUS

environs of our great cities, or indeed,

and more frequently, in the colonies.

However there is no reason

why the apparent advantages

OF THE ATTACKER

may not quickly be dissipated by a

prompt and precisely delivered

RESPONSE, REGARDLESS

of the ferocity or strength

OF THE OPPONENT.

2

How to escape WHEN attacked from the rear

How to overthrow *an assailant* who *attacks* you from **behind and pinions your arms:** method 1

Suppose that you are suddenly and unexpectedly attacked from behind in some lonely spot, finding a strong pair of arms encircling your body, so that your own arms are pinioned to your sides. Your position might appear at first sight to be utterly helpless — you might suppose that unless you were able to free yourself by struggling and kicking, nothing could save you from being thrown upon your back. However, by carrying out the following instructions, you will find that it is your assailant, and not yourself, who will be lying on his back before too many seconds have passed.

First, when finding your arms pinioned at your sides, bend forward and force your elbows outwards and upwards *(Fig. 1)*. Make yourself shorter by bending your knees, so as to cause your attacker's hold to slip over your shoulders *(Fig. 2)*. Then free your arms. You will probably find no difficulty in executing this movement. Having loosened his hold, you seize his right wrist with your left hand and the shoulder of his coat with your right hand, dropping at the same time onto your right knee and pulling him over your right shoulder, accompanying the movement with a right-to-left swing of the body *(Fig. 3)*. You thus deposit your adversary with a heavy thud on his back before you *(Fig. 4)*.

☞ "THIS FEAT IS A PARTICULARLY

NEAT PERFORMANCE

and in every way satisfactory

in case of the emergency I have described."

Fig. 1

Fig. 2

Fig. 3

Fig. 4

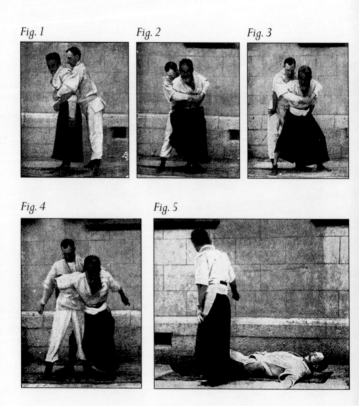

Fig. 1 Fig. 2 Fig. 3

Fig. 4 Fig. 5

How to overthrow *an assailant* who *attacks* you from **behind and pinions your arms:** method 2

It might be supposed that if a man were attacked from behind, and found that his assailant had pinioned his arms, it would be a difficult matter for him to release himself. This, however, is by no means the case, and by carefully following the instructions below it will be seen that it is a simple feat for a man not only to release himself when attacked in the manner described, but also to throw his assailant heavily to the ground without exerting any extraordinary strength.

(Fig. 1&2) Directly your arms are pinioned, raise your right foot and stamp heavily on your assailant's right foot. This immediately causes him to draw it back, in order to keep out of range of further danger.

(Fig. 3) You then grasp his right leg with your right hand, exerting as much pressure as possible with your thumb. By this means you will cause your opponent such pain that he will instinctively loosen his hold.

(Fig. 4) You immediately take advantage of this opportunity to place your right arm around his body, and your right leg behind his knee.

(Fig. 5) Then, striking him behind the knee with the inside of your leg, and accompanying the movement with a left-to-right swing of your body, you cause him to lose his balance, and throw him heavily upon his back.

One of the *many ways* to release yourself when *seized* by the **coat collar from behind**

PERHAPS ONE OF THE MOST DISCOMFITING FORMS OF ATTACK *is that in which an assailant makes a rush at his victim from behind and seizes him by the collar of his coat. Were you attacked in this way you might suppose that your position rendered you helpless, that the advantage was all on your adversary's side, that you could not use your hands with any great effect, and that you would probably be hurled at once onto your back.*

In order to avoid this mischance, you must act promptly. Directly you are seized by the collar, turn round and face your assailant, seizing him just behind the elbow, with the thumb and finger of your left hand. Then exert pressure on the nerve of the funny bone which is situated just behind the elbow. This will cause your assailant unendurable pain and he will immediately release his hold. Then, without releasing your hold, throw his arm upward with your left hand, step forward with your right foot, and place it behind his right leg. It will then be found to be a comparatively simple matter to seize him by the throat with your right hand and throw him upon his back.

☞ "Exerting pressure on the nerve of the funny bone will cause your assailant unendurable pain and he will immediately release his hold."

How to lift a chair *with four men* **packed upon it**

THE ATTENTIVE READER WILL HAVE OBSERVED my repeated statements that great strength is not a requisite for the mastery of this system of self-defence, and that the principles of balance and leverage are the key to its successful prosecution. This can be demonstrated through the brief exposition of various apparent feats of strength, which are in fact nothing of the sort. This trick demonstrates the truth of this assertion.

The first man, sitting in a natural position upon the chair must grasp the back legs as firmly as possible. Another man sits across his legs, facing him, and grasps the back of the chair. Two others are then placed lengthwise between these two, facing downwards. The chair is lifted in three stages. First, by charging the back with your shoulder you tilt it forward, so that everyone loses their balance, and the bottom man finds himself forced off the seat into a sitting position, and lifting the chair with the three men on his thighs. Then you push the chair forward by using your leg as a fulcrum against the crossbar, and make the seat strike number 1 man behind the knees. He will lose his balance and drop into the chair. Then you draw your leg away, and pull the chair backwards. The bottom man's feet will temporarily leave the ground, and you will thus produce the illusion of having lifted all four men into the air.

☞ "IT MUST NOT BE SUPPOSED THAT *it is necessary to possess unusual strength to* POSE AS A STRONG MAN; *indeed, in many strong men's feats* STRENGTH PLAYS A LESS IMPORTANT *part than knack and trickery.*"

☞ YOUR OUTER GARMENTS OFFER
A READY HAND-HOLD
for pickpockets and footpads,
who can thereby engage you at
close quarters, so that a swinging
BLOW IS RENDERED
IMPOSSIBLE OF EXECUTION.
Allowing this to be so, it is nonetheless
a simple matter to extricate yourself
from even the tightest grip,
through the astute application
OF THE PRINCIPLES
that underpin this system of self-defence.

3

How to escape when SEIZED
by an item of apparel

How to overcome an assailant *who seizes you by the waistbelt*, or attempts **to grasp the pocket of your coat:** method 1

To lay upon his back, in the space of a few seconds, an assailant who seizes you by the waist, four simple movements are necessary.

(Fig. 1) First you seize his right wrist with your left hand.

(Fig. 2) Secondly, you take a step to the side with your right foot, and strike him hard on the side of the head with your right fist, using the punch which is called by the Japanese uraken.

(Fig. 3) While your opponent is stunned, place your right leg behind his right knee, at the same time pushing firmly on his right shoulder.

(Fig. 4) Unbalanced, your assailant will be thrown ignominiously onto his back.

☞ "THE EFFECT WILL BE VERY
DISASTROUS TO YOUR
assailant, who will be completely at your mercy."

Fig. 1

Fig. 2

Fig. 3

Fig. 4

Fig. 1

Fig. 2

Fig. 3

Fig. 4

How to overcome an assailant *who seizes you by the waistbelt*, or attempts **to grasp the pocket of your coat:** method 2

HERE IS ANOTHER PRETTY WAY OF DEFENDING YOURSELF, and overthrowing an assailant who attempts to seize you by the pocket of your coat.

(Fig. 1) We will suppose that he makes his attack with his right hand. With your left hand firmly seize his right wrist.

(Fig. 2) Then seize his throat with your right hand, forcing your thumb into his tonsil. This will cause intense pain, and he will bend his head and body backwards in order to avoid it.

(Fig. 3) As before, place your right leg behind his right knee, at the same time pushing firmly on his right shoulder.

(Fig. 4) The result is the same, your assailant thrown onto his back and at the mercy of whatever punishment you see fit to apply to him.

How to disengage yourself and *overthrow an assailant* who seizes you by the **lappet of your coat** with his right hand

YOUR ASSAILANT SEIZES YOU WITH HIS RIGHT HAND, perhaps intending to snatch your watch with his left. You desire not only to frustrate his design, but to lay him on his back with as little trouble as possible in order that he shall not escape you, and may be duly handed over to the police. You will find the following method will meet your requirements.

(Fig. 1) Directly he seizes you, grasp his right wrist with your left hand, the outside of your hand being upward or on the top, and your thumb underneath his wrist.

(Fig. 2) Then take a step sideways with your left foot and slightly forwards, so that with another step you can place your right foot well behind his right leg. As soon as you have stepped onto one side, turn yourself half sideways and strike him with your right fist behind the ear.

Fig. 1

Fig. 2

Fig. 3

Fig. 4

Fig. 5

☞ "THIS SERIES OF MOVEMENTS MUST, *of course, be performed as quickly and* AS NEATLY AS POSSIBLE."

How to disengage yourself and *overthrow
an assailant* **who seizes you** by the **lappet
of your coat** with his right hand: CONTINUED

(Fig. 3) When he is off balance, but not before, follow
up the motion by placing your right leg quickly behind
his right leg. Then bear down on the upper part of his
arm, commencing at the shoulder, and ending at the
elbow, with the outside part of your forearm.

(Fig. 4) While you are doing this you retain a firm hold
of his right wrist with your left hand.

(Fig. 5) Pulling him towards you with your left hand,
and leaning over his right arm with your body, you
cause him to lose his balance and by this means he
will be easily thrown upon his back.

When seized by the *lappets of your coat,* **how to release yourself** and overthrow *your assailant*

WHEN A MAN SEIZES YOU BY THE LAPPETS OF YOUR COAT, he overlooks the fact that in this method of attack his face is left undefended. Your first movement will be therefore to strike him in the face with your right fist. This advice may seem unnecessary. It is not, however, so often followed, for the chances are that, when the occasion arises to which it applies, you will follow the natural and instinctive desire to free yourself by placing your hands upon your opponent's arms, and pressing upon them, which is as feeble as it is an unavailing method of resistance.

Remember, then, that your first movement should be to strike your assailant in the face with your right fist. If this does not cause him to release his hold, follow up the movement by passing your right forearm between his outstretched hands, and bring your right forearm up on the outer side of his right forearm. Then grasp your own right wrist with your left hand, and with the leverage thus obtained you may easily force his arm upwards and break his hold. The movement of breaking the hold should be made with suddenness and a quick jerk if your opponent be a powerful man with a strong grip. He will then be partially turned round. Take the opportunity to place your left leg behind him, and passing your left forearm across his chest, and seizing his left leg, you proceed to tip him over backwards.

☞ "Should a man seize you by the lappets of your coat, your first movement should be to strike him in the face with your right fist."

☞ "A SEVERE SHAKING IS A GREAT AND *terrible punishment, as those who have been* SO UNFORTUNATE AS TO *have experienced it will testify."*

Fig. 1

Fig. 2

Fig. 3

Fig. 4

If a man seizes you by the coat and ***attempts to shake you*** – how to release yourself and **overthrow your assailant**

IT IS VERY HUMILIATING TO BE SHAKEN. It is also very unpleasant. And it is a method of attack that is by no means uncommon, being especially resorted to by strong, big men, who pride themselves upon their strength and weight, and hesitate to strike a small man in case it be thought cowardly. It is well, therefore, to know how to overcome an opponent who seizes you by the coat and attempts to shake you.

(Fig. 1) Directly you are seized, strike your assailant simultaneously with both fists, in the face.

(Fig. 2) Bring your elbows down very sharply upon his wrists, which will have the effect of breaking his hold and jerking his head slightly forwards and downwards for a moment.

(Fig. 3) You immediately take this opportunity to catch him by the head, placing your right hand behind his head and the hollow of your left hand under his chin.

(Fig. 4) Then, stepping towards him with your left foot, and bringing your right foot behind your left foot (which acts as a sort of pivot to enable you to transmit a circular motion or twist to the neck), you throw him heavily upon his back.

"Sherlock Holmes seldom took exercise
for exercise's sake. Few men were capable of
greater muscular effort, and he was undoubtedly
one of the finest boxers of his weight that I have
ever seen; but he looked upon aimless bodily
exertion as a waste of energy, and seldom
bestirred himself save where there was some
professional object to be served."

Sir Arthur Conan Doyle, *The Yellow Face* (1893)

WHILE IT MAY BE CONSIDERED
a perfectly straightforward
matter to deal with an armed assailant
when you are yourself carrying
a stick, it should be remembered
THAT SUCH A FELLOW,
BY VIRTUE OF HIS HAVING
accepted the apparent disadvantage,
is likely to be an expert at his business.
This being the case, you should
treat such an opponent with
THE UTMOST REGARD,
whether it should happen that
you yourself are armed or not.

4

DEFENCE *against an* unarmed opponent

One of many ways to *defend yourself when a man strikes* at your **face with his right fist**

THIS IS A MOST USEFUL FEAT, AND THE STUDENT OF THE NEW ART of self-defence will do well to understand it thoroughly. We are assuming that your assailant begins his attack by attempting to strike you in the face.

Guard the blow by receiving it on your right forearm *(Fig. 1)*. Slip your hand up your assailant's arm, and grasp him by the wrist with finger and thumb, at the same time pulling him slightly forwards and seizing him by the elbow with your left hand *(Fig. 2)*. He will instinctively resist when you are pulling him towards you with your right hand *(Fig. 3)*. You take advantage of this moment to reverse the motion and bend his arm backwards *(Fig. 4)*. You then step forward and place your right leg behind his right leg and, pushing his elbow in an inward and upward direction, and his hand in an outward and downward direction, you cause him such pain that he is obliged to fall over backwards *(Fig. 5)*. Retaining your hold, you keep him down on the ground in this position and so great is your power that if you wished you could now break his arm *(Fig. 6)*.

Fig. 1

Fig. 2

Fig. 3

Fig. 4

Fig. 5

Fig. 6

☞ "THIS TRICK IS ENTIRELY DEPENDENT UPON THE QUICKNESS OF *the eye in judging the right moment* TO JUMP TO ONE SIDE."

Fig. 1

Fig. 2

A very safe way to *disable a boxer who attempts* to rush you when you **are armed with a stick**

IMAGINE THE CASE OF A MAN ARMED WITH A SERVICEABLE STICK being attacked by a skilled boxer. One of the safest and most reliable methods of defence against a boxer's fists is as follows.

(Fig. 1) Face the boxer with your left foot and arm extended, and your right arm guarding your head. Your left arm is thus free to guard your face and body if, by any chance, you should fail to evade the blow.

(Fig. 2) As soon as the boxer opens his attack with a direct blow, jump forward, bending well forward in a crouching position so as to avoid any possibility of being hit.

A very safe way to *disable a boxer who attempts* to rush you when you **are armed with a stick:** CONTINUED

(Fig. 3) Then, turning half round on your left toe, and drawing your right foot in a line with your left, make a low, back-handed sweep with the stick, striking the boxer on his knee, disabling him and bringing him to the ground.

(Fig. 4) Suppose that, in the excitement of the engagement, your blow missed the boxer's knee and struck him on the shin, in which case he might still be able to show fight. Quickly recovering his balance, the boxer turns on his left toe and puts in another blow. Anticipating this movement, you then bayonette the boxer in the heart before the blow can fall. Since the stick gives you a longer reach than the boxer, there is no danger, and the strong upward thrust of your stick should completely incapacitate your adversary.

Fig. 3

Fig. 4

Fig. 1

Fig. 2

Fig. 3

How to defend yourself *with a stick* against the **most dangerous kick of an expert kicker**

You might suppose that there would be no great difficulty in guarding against a high kick, provided you carried a stout stick in your hand. Those who have seen foot-boxers at work, however, and realise the swiftness of the kicks which they plant on their opponents' bodies, will understand that scientific kicking can only be guarded against with certainty by a scientific method of defence.

Taking up a position of rear-guard, with left arm extended to ward off a possible kick at the small of the back, hip or left side, you describe circular cuts in a left-to-right downward direction with your stick *(Fig. 1)*. Your opponent prepares to do what in French boxing is called a chassé – that is, from his original position, with his left foot and left arm extended, he places his right foot behind his left so as to enable him to approach within kicking distance if the opportunity presents itself *(Fig. 2)*. Then, seeing an opening, he places his right heel firmly on the ground and aims a kick with his foot at your heart. Anticipating the danger you transfer the whole weight of your body from your left to your right leg, which enables you at the critical moment to withdraw your foot very quickly, and at the same time assists you to draw your body out of danger *(Fig. 3)*. You then bring your stick down so heavily on your adversary's ankle as to break it.

The best way to ***disable a man*** who tries to ***rush you*** and get under your guard in order to prevent you **hitting him** with a **hooked stick**

AN ASSAILANT FACED WITH AN ARMED OPPONENT will indubitably attempt first to render the contest equal by disposing of his adversary's weapon. This trick effectively counters any such attempt.

(Fig. 1) Stand with your right leg forward and make a slight threatening motion with your left hand, as though you intend to seize the left hand of your assailant.

(Fig. 2) The object of the feint is only to engage your adversary's attention, and make him look at your left hand whilst you suddenly dart forward and hook him by the neck in the crook of your stick.

(Fig. 3) Directly you have hooked him, bend your knees well so as to throw the whole weight of your body upon him, whilst you pull him down with his face towards the ground.

Fig. 1

Fig. 2

Fig. 3

☞ "IT IS NECESSARY TO BE VERY CAREFUL WHEN PRACTISING THIS TRICK *as the slightest blow with the knee in a person's face is sufficient to break the* NOSE AND SEVERAL TEETH."

Fig. 4

Fig. 5

The best way to *disable a man* who tries to *rush you* and get under your guard in order to prevent you **hitting him** with a **hooked stick:**

(Fig. 4) When you have pulled him down sufficiently far to prevent him from recovering his balance quickly, let go of your stick and seize him by the shoulders, being careful to keep your feet well out of the reach of his hands, so as not to give him the opportunity of throwing you backwards.

(Fig. 5) Then, with a sudden jerk, pull him forwards, and simultaneously jumping close to him, strike him with your knee in the face.

A very simple way to *protect yourself* with a **hooked walking stick** against a boxer

WHEN CARRYING A HOOKED STICK, here is a very simple way to protect yourself against the attack of an unarmed assailant.

(Fig. 1) Hold your stick behind you, so as to run no risk of the stick-arm being seized. Bend your left arm with the inside of the left hand facing outwards in order to protect yourself from a kick at the hip, or a blow from the fist at your face or ribs.

(Fig. 2) At the moment when the boxer leads off, you must put your head well to one side and bend both knees quite considerably so as to get well under his guard. Directly you receive his blow on your arm, you must straighten your knees, and so throw up the boxer's arm, and make him lose his balance, which prevents him from using his right fist upon your ribs.

(Fig. 3) You now have the opportunity, and plenty of time, to hook him by the ankle with your stick.

(Fig. 4) Having so hooked his foot, pull his legs apart and bring him to the ground, where you can apply the stick when and how you please.

Fig. 1

Fig. 2

Fig. 3

Fig. 4

How to face a wall, *with your arms outstretched,* and defy any number of **strong men to push you against it**

A FURTHER DEMONSTRATION OF THE SUPERIORITY OF BALANCE and counter-movement against sheer force. Take up a position against the wall as shown. Be careful, however, to resist the power from behind entirely with your wrists, for if you attempt to resist with your hands only, they would be bent back, and your wrists, in all probability, would receive a severe strain.

The object of the people pressing behind you is to push you against the wall; your object is not so much to resist them as to break their line – a very simple matter as I shall show, if you know how. Arrange to have a weak man pressing immediately on your shoulder blades. Place two silk handkerchiefs, which are very slippery, upon your shoulders, saying that you take this precaution in order that your coat shall not be spoiled. Then, when the word is given, and everyone begins to push with all their power, it is not at all improbable that the weak man will give way before you feel any severe strain, and the line will naturally fall to pieces. However, if this does not happen, slightly bend one of your arms (the one furthest away from the audience), and lower your shoulder, causing the hand of the man immediately behind you to slip. Those pushing behind will lose their balance, and the line will be immediately broken. You then straighten your bent arm and assume the original position.

☞ "IN INTRODUCING A FURTHER SELECTION OF THESE FEATS, IT MAY BE AS *well to mention again the fact that there is not one among them that any person of* **AVERAGE STRENGTH COULD** NOT LEARN AND PERFORM."

☞ IN MASTERING THE ART OF SELF *defence with a stick it is important* to learn how you may best wield your weapon **with two hands, otherwise you** might be at serious disadvantage **WHEN CARRYING A HEAVY STICK** *which you could not use freely with one hand, if attacked by a man carrying a* **lighter cane with which he could** make quick, one-handed play.

USE OF *the stout* stick

Showing the best way to *handle with two hands* a stick which is *too heavy to manipulate* quickly with one hand, when attacked by a **man armed with a light stick**

THE PREPARATORY POSITION FOR DELIVERING a double-handed blow at your adversary's head is a position of guard, in which you hold the stick with both hands horizontally above your head, with thumbs away from your face and hands at the ends of the stick. The beauty of this position lies in the fact that your opponent does not know which end of the stick you intend to use to hit him with.

We will suppose that you are holding the stick with the heaviest end in your right hand, and that you propose to hit him with this end *(Fig. 1)*. The blow is delivered thus – you slide your right hand quickly off the right-hand end of the stick, and bring it back again, holding the stick with the thumb on the side nearest your face. Then, using your left hand as a pivot, you slide your right hand up to your left with a circular motion, thus delivering a strong side blow at your adversary's face *(Fig. 2)*. Should you wish to strike your opponent with the opposite end of the stick – the lighter end – you would slip your left hand off the left end of the stick, bring it back with the thumb on the side nearest your face, and then slide your left hand towards your right, to impart a circular motion to the stick as before.

☞ "A PERSON REQUIRES TO BE VERY SUPPLE *in the shoulders to work a stick* gracefully and well with two hands."

Fig. 1

Fig. 2

Fig. 1

Fig. 2

A safe way *for one man to disable another* when both are **equally well armed with sticks**

Supposing that you are attacked by a man armed, like yourself, with a stout stick, here is a very pretty way to disable him.

(Fig. 1) Standing in the position of front guard, right foot forward, knees bent, right arm extended, you invite an attack at your head by holding your guard rather low. Your opponent accepts the invitation, and leads off at your head.

(Fig. 2) You parry – an easy matter, as you are prepared for this blow.

A safe way *for one man to disable another* when both are **equally well armed with sticks:** CONTINUED

(Fig. 3) Simultaneously jumping well to your opponent's right, you crouch down and make a low, sweeping cut at his knees, which will bring him to the ground.

(Fig. 4) If, however, by any chance this result is not achieved, because your blow has fallen upon your opponent's shin instead of upon his knee, you will still have the best of the situation. Finding that you have got under his guard, your adversary will draw back his right foot and prepare to give you a back-handed cut across the face. You, however, foil this attempt by keeping too close to him to admit of this, and bayonette him with the point of your stick.

☞ "I SPECIALLY RECOMMEND THIS TO THE *attention of the reader, whether* lady or gentleman, as being both very EASY AND MOST EFFECTIVE."

Fig. 3

Fig. 4

Fig. 1

Fig. 2

Fig. 3

The safest way to **meet an attack with a spiked staff or long stick** when you are only armed with **an ordinary walking-stick**

In this case the man armed with the staff has the advantage of reach, which must be countered by the greater agility of his more lightly armed opponent.

Figure 1 shows the most dangerous mode of attack with a long stick, and also the best position to adopt in order to meet such an attack with safety. It will be seen that the figure on the right is exposing his body in order to ensure his adversary's attacking him there, and to be prepared with an immediate defence. Directly the man with the alpenstock attempts to bayonette him, he diverts the blow by turning sideways, and making a circular downward cut, which hits the alpenstock and causes it to glide slightly upwards and sideways – a guard known in sword-play as Septime envelopé *(Fig. 2)*. The moment the blow has been diverted, the man with the stick must seize the alpenstock with his left hand, and, stepping in, strike his assailant a blow across the face *(Fig. 3)*.

An example of a *very pretty guard and counter-blow* when an assailant aims a **blow at your head with a stick**

As I have stated elsewhere, it is always most desirable to try *to entice your adversary to deliver a certain blow, and so place yourself at a great advantage by being prepared to guard it, and to deliver your counter-blow.*

(Fig. 1) Directly you have had time to catch your opponent's eye and judge your striking distance, you must expose your head, either by slightly lowering your guard, or by holding your hand and stick well on one side, so as to invite an attack on your head.

(Fig. 2) When your assailant attempts to strike you on the head with his stick, you may receive the blow upon your stick by bringing your hand right across your face, and holding it well on the left side of your head with the back of your hand outwards, facing your opponent. Your stick should point slightly downwards to prevent your opponent's stick sliding down yours, and striking you on the fingers.

(Fig. 3) The moment you have done this you step slightly towards your opponent's right side with your right foot, and describe a circular left-to-right back-handed cut across his face, which should be sufficient to prevent him troubling you any further.

☞ "BESIDES BEING A MOST USEFUL AND PRACTICAL *accomplishment, this new art of* self~defence with a walking~stick is to be RECOMMENDED AS A MOST *exhilarating and graceful exercise.*"

Fig. 1

Fig. 2

Fig. 3

Fig. 1

Fig. 2

Fig. 3

Examples of the *double-handed guard* in **combination with ambidexterity**

It will be evident that, in order for an effective defence to be maintained in stick-play, the skilled exponent will require to be equally proficient with either hand.

(Fig. 1) In this example the man on the left is seen taking up the double-handed guard, but his assailant refuses to accept the invitation at his body, although it is exposed – instead of this he aims a blow at the left wrist, or the left side of the head.

(Fig. 2) On this, the man with the double-handed guard, in order to avoid being hit upon the fingers, lets go of the left-hand end of his stick, and swings his left hand behind him – a movement which automatically imparts the initial movement for a right-handed blow. This he delivers across his opponent's wrist, which he would thus break, just as the assailant is in the act of striking.

(Fig. 3) In this example, the defender, as before, invites an attack at his body by guarding his head in an exaggerated way. His opponent immediately attempts to take advantage of the opening by striking at the exposed body, when the other simply draws his left foot towards his right, and so retires out of striking distance of his adversary. Then, by releasing his hold on the stick with his right hand, he brings it down heavily with his left upon his assailant's head.

How, when *lying down at full length* on two chair backs placed at your extremities, **to support a person standing on your chest**

I ADVISE ONLY THE STRONGER SECTION OF MY READERS to attempt this trick; it is not a case of trickery so much as a case of strength, though less strength is required than anyone would imagine who first witnesses the performance.

Have two chairs placed in such positions that, when you are lying horizontally, the back of one will support your shoulders, and the back of the other your feet. Then ask your friends to tie your arms lightly to your sides, a device which gives invaluable support.

On the top of the chair on which your shoulders will rest place a thick overcoat, doubled twice. This, it will be found, will extend the support, not only down your back, but up your legs. It will, in fact, have the same effect as would a flat board.

Lie at length on the ground, and request two people to take you up, one by the legs and the other by the head, and to place you on the chairs. They should sit upon the chairs as ballast. Arrange for someone to step upon your chest from another chair at a given signal. Then, when everything is ready, draw a long breath, give the signal, and when the ordeal is over try to assume as pleasant a look as possible.

☞ "ALTHOUGH THE MAJORITY OF THESE FEATS *are of so simple a nature as to* be readily understood, it is as well to PRACTISE THEM BEFORE *venturing on a public performance."*

☞ WITH REFERENCE TO THIS SHORT description of walking-stick play, *I may state that the art of self-defence* **with a walking-stick is particularly** adapted to conditions where a man IS ATTACKED BY MORE **THAN ONE PERSON. IT CAN BE** *readily acquired, either by men or women, and once mastered would* **enable you to defend yourself,** **WITH ABSOLUTE SAFETY,** against a knife, boxing, savate, etc. *The more dangerous methods* HAVE NOT BEEN SHOWN.

6

USE OF THE *short stick*

or umbrella

The *guard* by **distance**

*IT WILL BE NOTICED THAT IN THIS METHOD OF DEFENCE the man
attacked does not attempt to guard a blow by raising his hands
to stop it, but simply by changing front from left to right foot.
By so doing, he avoids being hit himself, with the certainty of
being able to hit his adversary.*

When guarding by distance, you take up the position
of rear-guard – that is to say, you stand with left foot
forward, slightly bent knees, right arm held above
the head, and left arm thrown well out in front of
you *(Fig. 1)*. You must be careful to maintain the
same distance between yourself and your adversary,
by retiring as he advances, and advancing as he retires.
Your opponent, encouraged by the apparently exposed
position of your left arm, naturally strikes at it, but you
withdraw it very quickly, and swing it upwards behind
you. This upward sweep of the arm automatically causes
you to swing your left foot well behind your right, and
to draw in the lower part of your body out of your
opponent's reach; at the same time it imparts the initial
momentum to your right arm, and assists in bringing
your stick down very quickly and heavily upon your
adversary's head *(Fig. 2)*.

Fig. 1

Fig. 2

Fig. 3

Fig. 4

The *guard* by **distance:** CONTINUED

To induce your opponent to aim a blow at your
head you take up the same position of rear-guard,
but instead of exposing your arm so much, you push
your head more forward, leaving it apparently quite
unguarded *(Fig. 3)*. Your assailant foolishly accepts the
invitation, and you promptly draw yourself out of
danger by swinging your left foot behind your right.
This movement gives an automatic counter-movement
to the right side of your trunk and helps you to swing
a very heavy right-handed blow across his wrist,
which might thus easily be broken *(Fig. 4)*.

How to *defend yourself* when your adversary is armed with a *stout stick* and you are **carrying only a light cane**

IMAGINE THAT YOU ARE WALKING IN A LONELY PART of the country, carrying a light switch or an umbrella, when suddenly a footpad bars your way, carrying a stout stick, with which he threatens you.

(Fig. 1) Appreciating the unreliability of your weapon, you assume the offensive at once before your opponent has time to discover your disadvantage.

(Fig. 2) You begin operations by striking high at your assailant's head, and forcing him to guard high.

(Fig. 3) Simultaneously you spring forward, seizing your opponent just below the elbow, thereby completely disturbing his balance, and so preventing him from hitting you. You can now deliver a heavy right-handed blow with your fist upon his chin, or over his heart, which will render him unconscious.

(Fig. 4) In case you are carrying a stick which might be strong enough to deliver a heavy blow, another method of attack is as follows: After you have disturbed your assailant's balance by seizing him by the elbow, you retire quickly, by withdrawing your left foot well behind your right, and then, holding your head and body well on one side out of possible danger, you deliver a heavy blow with your stick across your assailant's kneecap.

Fig. 1

Fig. 2

Fig. 3

Fig. 4

☞ "OF COURSE, IT IS UNDERSTOOD THAT IF *the tall man has only got a weak* STICK OR UMBRELLA IN HIS HAND, *directly he obtained the advantage shown* **in Fig. 2, he would use his fist to** STRIKE HIS OPPONENT IN THE FACE."

Fig. 1

Fig. 2

Fig. 3

One of the ***safest plans of defence*** for a tall man to adopt who has ***not much* confidence** in his own quickness and knowledge of ***stick-play,*** when opposed by a **shorter and more competent opponent**

A TALL, SLOW-MOVING MAN, ATTACKED BY A QUICK, short opponent, is at an immense disadvantage, as the short man delivers his attacks at lightning speed in unexpected quarters, and so reduces any possible advantage the other may hold in size and reach. Under the circumstances it would be advisable for the tall man to try to induce his opponent to deliver a blow for which he will be fully prepared.

(Fig. 1) This he will best do by taking up the rear-guard position, as previously described. He then throws his left arm forward as a bait. In ninety-nine cases out of a hundred the bait will prove irresistible.

(Fig. 2) No sooner, however, does the short man begin to move his stick, with the intention of bringing it across the tall man's arm, than the latter must jump within the former's guard, in order to break the force of his blow as it falls.

(Fig. 3) Then seizing the other's stick, the tall man can belabour his opponent's head.

One of the **best ways of knocking down**
a man in a general scrimmage when there is
not room to swing a stick freely

WHEN A MAN FINDS IT NECESSARY TO DEFEND HIMSELF in a street
fight, or the like, he may not have room to swing a stick freely.
One of the best methods of using a stick as a weapon under
these circumstances is as follows.

In order to carry out the trick effectively on a single
assailant, when there is no crowd, you should stand in
the front-guard position, and make a cut at the side of
your opponent's face *(Fig. 1)*. While he raises his hand to
guard his face, you seize his uplifted hand with your left
hand, crouch down and pass your stick through his legs
(Fig. 2). Pressing your stick sharply against the inside of
one of his thighs, you then exert sufficient leverage to
throw him on his back *(Fig. 3)*.

☞ "To employ the same trick in a crowd *it is only necessary to stoop, cover* YOUR FACE WELL WITH YOUR ARM *and hand, and to keep diving with your stick* **between people's legs, upsetting** THEM RIGHT AND LEFT."

Fig. 1

Fig. 2

Fig. 3

Fig. 1

Fig. 2

Fig. 3

Fig. 4

Fig. 5

An effective way *to defend yourself* with a *hooked stick* when attacked by a man **armed with an ordinary straight stick**

Suppose that you are carrying a crooked stick when you are suddenly attacked by an assailant armed with an ordinary straight stick. Here is a very pretty way to overthrow the assailant.

(Fig. 1) In the first place, you should hold your hand and stick high up, and well on one side, so as not to run any risk of being hit on the fingers. By doing this, you purposely expose your head to attack.

(Fig. 2) Knowing, therefore, that your opponent is sure to strike at your head, you are prepared for a quick guard. The attacker delivers his blow and is received upon the stick.

(Fig. 3) Before he has time to recover himself, and get into a position of defence, you suddenly duck and hook him by the foot, on the outer side of the ankle.

(Fig. 4) By pulling his legs apart you can then bring him to the ground.

(Fig. 5) The assailant is then at your mercy, and you can choose any part of his body on which to administer a suitable punishment.

One of the ***best ways to meet*** a direct attack upon the head with a **very heavy stick** when armed with **an ordinary stick**

IN COMBATING THE ATTACK OF AN ADVERSARY ARMED with a stouter stick than your own, you must take advantage of the greater speed and precision afforded by your own weapon to counter the superior weight of your opponent's.

Figure 1 shows a man armed with a heavy stick in the act of striking at the head of a man armed with a walking-stick. The latter is standing in the double-handed position of guard; and it will be noticed that in holding his weapon he places his hands so that the back of his left hand is on the side nearest his face, and the back of his right hand on the side farthest from his face; in other words, the positions of his hands are reversed. Directly the assailant delivers his blow, the man with the walking-stick slides his stick through his right hand until his hands meet, and then twists the stick without altering his hold in any way so that his right hand passes over his left. In this position, with his wrists crossed, he holds the stick above his head, to receive the downward cut delivered by his adversary *(Fig. 2)*.

Fig. 1

Fig. 2

Fig. 3

Fig. 4

Fig. 5

One of the *best ways to meet* a direct attack
upon the head with a **very heavy stick** when
armed with **an ordinary stick:** CONTINUED

Directly he has guarded the blow, and so broken the
force of it, letting go the stick with the left hand, with
this hand he seizes the assailant's staff. Retaining hold
of the stick with his right hand, the man attacked may
then break his opponent's wrist with a heavy blow
(Fig. 3). Another method is to let the blow fall across
the assailant's kneecap *(Fig. 4).* Still another way to
proceed is for the man attacked to continue to use his
own weapon with both hands, and to deliver a heavy
blow across his adversary's face *(Fig. 5).*

"Sherlock Holmes had sprung out and seized the intruder by the collar. The other dived down the hole and I heard the sound of rending cloth as Jones clutched at his skirts. The light flashed upon the barrel of a revolver, but Holmes's hunting-crop came down upon the man's wrist, and the pistol clinked upon the stone floor.

'It's no use, John Clay,' said Holmes blandly; 'you have no chance at all.'"

Sir Arthur Conan Doyle, *The Red-Headed League* (1891)

☞ AS I HAVE STATED PREVIOUSLY, *the aim of this new system of* self-defence is to minimise the need for **brute strength in dealing** WITH AN OPPONENT. Speed is of the essence, since the **MORE EXPEDITIOUSLY THE** situation is dealt with, the less likely it is that you will be required to employ **MORE EXTREME METHODS.** It will be found that an adversary who is promptly **DEPOSITED UPON HIS BACK** *is unlikely to be capable of any* FURTHER UNPLEASANTNESS.

7

How to *throw and hold*

a man upon the ground

One of many ways to *throw a man,* without exerting strength, **when you seize him from behind**

Suppose the case that a ruffian is threatening one of your companions, you at this moment being behind the attacker.

Seize the man by the collar of his coat from behind, and place your foot behind his knee. Pull with your hand, and press with your foot, and he will be at once deposited upon his back!

Without releasing your hold upon his collar, pass your right hand around his neck, so that you can bring your forearm across his throat. Then, seizing the right lappet of his coat with your left hand to prevent the coat from moving, you bear down with all your weight across his wind-pipe with your right arm, and so render him powerless to resist, and – if need be – throttle him!

WHEN CONSIDERING THE ADVA

is new art of self-def

st be remembered that

nes when no method is too

E ADOPTED IN OR

VERTHROW AN ASSAIL.

Fig. 1

Fig. 2

Fig. 3

How to *overcome an assailant* who seizes **both your wrists**

IN THIS CASE WE WILL SUPPOSE THAT YOU ARE SUDDENLY attacked in such a way that both your wrists are held captive by your assailant. The advantage is, of course, with him, but he will, however, be easily overthrown, if the following tactics are carried out.

Your assailant will probably face you with his right foot forward. In this respect you follow his example *(Fig. 1)*. Then, seize his left wrist with your left hand; release your right wrist by pushing your arm suddenly downwards. Seize your opponent's right wrist with your released right hand, and, with a jerk downwards, cause him to release his hold of your left wrist. As soon as you have done this, draw his right arm over his left forearm, so that the back of the elbow passes across the centre of his left arm *(Fig. 2)*. Follow up the movement by raising his left arm, and bearing down upon his right arm. The result will be instantaneous, and very surprising to your opponent, who will be forced to turn a somersault in the air, and will fall heavily on his back *(Fig. 3)*. Still retaining your hold on his wrists, you will now have him completely at your mercy.

How to *hold a man* upon the ground in such *a position* that he is **unable to move**

HAVING ONCE DEPOSITED YOUR ADVERSARY UPON HIS BACK, there may well be circumstances in which you will require to keep him under your power until such time as the police or other official authorities arrive at the scene. Such a method as the following will be found to be perfectly serviceable.

(Fig. 1) As promptly as possible, seize your opponent's foot. Then, if you twist it smartly in the way indicated, you will find no difficulty in turning him on his face.

(Fig. 2) Immediately this has been done, release the hold of one hand, and place your forearm tightly behind his knee. Then, by forcing the foot backwards, you can exert such leverage that if your opponent should still attempt to resist, you could break both his knee and his ankle.

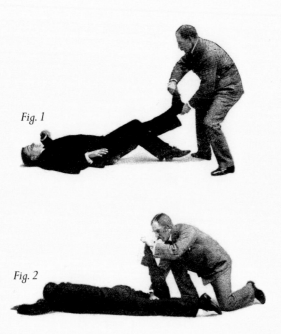

Fig. 1

Fig. 2

Fig. 1

Fig. 2

Fig. 3

Fig. 4

Fig. 5

How to *overcome a ruffian* who attacks you **with a knife**

I MAY STATE THAT I HAVE REPEATEDLY BEEN ATTACKED during a long residence in Portugal by men with a knife or six-foot quarter-staff, and have in all cases succeeded in disabling my adversary without being hurt myself.

Carry your overcoat upon your shoulders, in the style of a military cloak, with your right hand ready upon your left shoulder *(Fig. 1)*. Directly your assailant attacks, face him and wait until he is within a distance of two or three yards. Then envelop his head and arms by throwing your coat at him, with a sweeping, circular motion of the arm *(Fig. 2)*. This will obscure his view momentarily, and will give you plenty of time to deliver your attack *(Fig. 3)*. While he is still enveloped in the folds of your coat, slip round behind him, seize him by the right ankle, and push him under the shoulder blade with your left hand *(Fig. 4)*. You will thus throw him very violently upon his face, and in his endeavour to break his fall and protect his face he will put out his hands, and involuntarily drop his weapon *(Fig. 5)*. He will then be disarmed and in a position where you can break his leg immediately if you so like.

How to *overcome an assailant* who seizes you **by the right arm**

THIS IS A VERY PRETTY AND EFFECTUAL METHOD OF overthrowing an assailant who seizes you by the right wrist with both hands.

(Fig. 1) As soon as your arm is seized, you raise your hand in front of your chest towards your left shoulder. But, if your opponent is too heavy and strong to admit of your doing this, you must step slightly towards him with your right foot and bend your knees sufficiently to admit of your hand being nearly level with your left shoulder.

(Fig. 2) Directly this stage has been reached, rearrange your feet in such a way that you may exert your strength to the best advantage in the direction you desire – i.e., so that you may easily throw your assailant off with a sweep of the arm. But before using your strength, bend your knees well in order to be well under your work. Then, with a vigorous movement of your arms, accompanied by the lifting motion supplied by straightening your knees, you throw him off his balance and turn him partly round, so that your right hand comes in front of his face.

Fig. 1

Fig. 2

Fig. 3

Fig. 4

How to *overcome an assailant* who seizes you **by the right arm:** CONTINUED

(Fig. 3) Now take a strong step behind him with your left foot, seize him by the chin with your right hand, and by the back of the head with your left hand.

(Fig. 4) Then, by bringing your left foot back again with a long stride behind your right, you impart a circular twist to your assailant's head and neck, which will throw him heavily upon his back.

"'Not Mr Sherlock Holmes!' roared the prize-fighter. 'God's truth! How could I have mistook you? If instead o' standing there so quiet you had just stepped up and given me that cross-hit of yours under the jaw, I'd ha' known you without a question. Ah, you're one that has wasted your gifts, you have! You might have aimed high, if you had joined the fancy.'

'You see, Watson, if all else fails me, I still have one of the scientific professions open to me,' said Holmes, laughing."

Sir Arthur Conan Doyle, *The Sign of Four* (1890)

by leaders who are tempted to consider this appendix frivolous, I would draw attention to the following particulars. A cyclist is potentially EASY PREY FOR A HIGHWAY robber. His conveyance may be upset quite easily — a stick in the SPOKES OF HIS WHEEL, A SUDDEN jerk to the handle-bars, and he is thrown inevitably. However, the cyclist who is a skilful rider, WHO POSSESSES PLUCK AND DASH, and who is armed with a knowledge of how to use a machine to the best advantage as a weapon, may rest CONTENT THAT HE IS ABLE to defend himself perfectly when attacked under the majority

8

SELF-DEFENCE *from a* bicycle

Repelling an *assailant who positions* himself in the **path of your bicycle**

Perhaps the commonest occasion when *a little knowledge of the art of self-defence when awheel would prove of greatest use is when a rider is menaced by a rough who blocks the road.*

A lady, say, is riding alone on a country road, when an approaching tramp suddenly assumes a hostile attitude, standing before her with legs apart and arms outstretched, effectively barring the way *(Fig. 1)*. Now this is the method for removing the tramp, and for riding past in safety. The lady should put on a spurt and ride, point blank, at her assailant. Certainly this requires nerve, but it is perfectly simple and effective. The tramp cannot overcome the instinct of self-protection which makes him jump to one side, when the cyclist, of course, at once swerves in the other direction *(Fig. 2)*. A simple means of defence that may be highly recommended for the use of lady cyclists is the water squirt. This is an ingenious weapon sold in cycling shops, made in the shape of a pistol, but with an india rubber handle which holds water, and which, when pressed, will squirt a shower of water for a distance of 20 feet or so. The footpad who attempted to approach a lady cyclist, and was met with a douche of cold water, would receive a severe shock that would cause him to stand back long enough to allow his intended victim to escape *(Fig. 3)*.

Fig. 1

Fig. 2

Fig. 3

Fig. 1

Fig. 2

How to *defend yourself with your bicycle* when accosted by a **ruffian at close quarters**

THERE ARE OCCASIONS WHEN IT IS SAFER, if attacked whilst cycling, to meet an assailant dismounted, rather than awheel. Here is a case in point.

You are riding along a country road, when suddenly you are startled by a man who springs in front of you from the hedge, and attempts to grab your machine. You should instantly spring backwards off your machine, and by pulling at the handle-bars, cause it to rear up on its back wheel *(Fig. 1)*. You are now face to face with your assailant, with your machine standing up perpendicularly before you. You may retain your hold of the handle-bars with both hands, or place your right hand on the saddle – in either case you have perfect control over your machine, and may run it backwards or forwards before you, to the right or to the left, as you desire. Your adversary will jump back from sheer surprise and thus lose his balance. Seizing this opportunity, you should take a sharp step forward, and hurl your machine at your assailant, letting it run on its back wheel, and so directing it as it leaves your hands that the front wheel will come heavily down on top of him *(Fig. 2)*. He will necessarily stagger backwards under the weight of the machine, whereupon you may make good your escape, or else offer him whatever physical punishment seems appropriate.

Using your *bicycle as a shield* when challenged by a **ruffian at close quarters**

HERE IS ANOTHER METHOD BY WHICH A BICYCLE may be utilised both as a shield and as a weapon.

(Fig. 1) You have dismounted, we will suppose, to meet on foot an unexpected attack. You should take care, under these circumstances, to place your machine between your assailant and yourself, holding it by the handle-bars. Then make your cycle describe a half-circle around you, with precisely the same movement as you would employ if you were using a scythe in a hay field.

(Fig. 2) As your assailant leads with his right arm you should duck beneath the blow, simultaneously twisting the handle-bars towards you. Then, after slightly altering the position of the bicycle frame so as to enclose the attacker's leading leg, you should push the handle-bars sharply away from you. This will result in your trapping his outstretched leg between the front wheel of the cycle and the sloping bar of the frame. By now turning the handle-bar with your left hand so that a strong pressure is exerted by the back of the front wheel against your assailant's leg, you cause him such pain that he is powerless to harm you.

(Fig. 3) You may now lean forward and strike him in the chest or face with your right fist.

☞ "THE VARIOUS MOVEMENTS BY WHICH THE HAPPY *termination of this incident is* brought about should be done with ONE SWIFT, STRONG, *comprehensive sweep of the cycle, and* **a blow which should follow** almost simultaneously, so that all will BE OVER IN A MOMENT."

Fig. 1

Fig. 2

Fig. 3

☞ "AFTERWARDS, WHEN YOU HAVE DEALT with your adversary, it is entirely *possible that you will find your* CYCLE LYING UNHARMED *on the road-side.*"

Fig. 1

Fig. 2

A direct *method of defence* when a narrow path is **blocked by a ruffian**

IT IS NOT ALWAYS POSSIBLE TO DEAL WITH AN assailant with so little danger to oneself as in the previous cases. In emergencies it will sometimes be found necessary to take calculated risks.

Suppose, for example, that you are riding along a narrow track, when suddenly a man bars your way *(Fig. 1)*. To turn and flee is impossible, and nor is there room to dismount and apply the tricks described earlier. In this case you should ride boldly up to your assailant, leap from your machine full upon him, and throw your arms around his neck, leaving your cycle to go where it pleases *(Fig. 2)*. You will come upon him with an irresistible momentum, as though you had dropped from the sky, and if you have not sufficiently damaged him when he strikes the ground, you have the advantage of now being on top, which advantage you may press home in any way you please.

Sir Arthur Conan Doyle
(1859–1930)